ABOUT THE AUTHOR

Mitchell Ritter is a New York City born, Swiss trained clinical/Jungian psychologist. He spent many years living, studying and working in Europe, and has been back in New York since 2002. Living and working on the Upper East Side, he has two grown daughters and two large dogs.

For further information, please refer to the following website where the author provides insightful quotations and observations on current psychological and social issues drawn from his clinical practice:

www.analyticalpsychologynyc.com

Comments, thoughts, questions are all welcome and can be addressed to:

analyticalpsychologynyc@gmail.com.

ACKNOWLEDGEMENTS

I have wanted to make this short story – a hybrid of fiction and case study – available to those many people who have found themselves in a situation where they were in love with someone who loved them as well, where all the elements were in place for a happy conclusion, only to see it fail. Often, no explanation is offered, and one is left to speculate as to the reasons. As a very indirect participant, I tried to recreate the conditions, and explain how wrong decisions get made when right ones are seemingly obvious, yet ultimately rejected.

I want to thank Augustine Iglesias for his thoughtful reading, energy and encouragement to publish this, and for his project management skills in getting this done. Without him, this would still probably be sitting on my computer.

And finally, Mr. Hide. We are no longer in contact so I don't know if he remained in his "prison," or locked into what he described himself as "the Stockholm Syndrome" – where the hostage comes to identify with the captor to the point that he cannot leave them. I wish him well.

Mr. Hide's Progress

Prologue

This is a work of fiction based on a story I was told as it was unfolding. It is first and foremost a love story – one of love found, discarded, found again, embraced and ultimately discarded once again – for all the wrong reasons. This last point became clear to me over the years since I first wrote it down, through discussions with my patients. It just seemed to come up as an excellent example when change – fundamental change – was in play. And so I came to see it just as importantly, as a parable about change in our lives. Like so many parables, it comes with a message.

Mr. Hide's Progress allowed me to follow the evolution of the underlying process – a very deeply human one, little discussed by the way – and the role "love" plays in our lives, well beyond the rather simplistic, not to say childish, view we have developed of love, for love serves many purposes – but only one Master.   I'll leave that discussion for the end of the story. Suffice it to say, as we have banalized love, we have weakened it, made it less relevant to our lives, and deprived ourselves of a true life force.

Coming back to the story, it was related to me through Mr. Hide, reflecting his situation, needs and perspective. Through his actions, words and choices, he was an eloquent spokesman for himself, and for those he ultimately sided with. Interestingly – and unintentionally, I'm certain - he allowed me to realize that it wasn't only his story. It was also the story of his lover who, though incarnating all that was "good" about love, revealed his own blindness, and therefore this somehow also became his story as well.

As in every love story, there is always more than one perspective. Perhaps it would have been more "objective" if I had heard the other side (in fact sides, for the Master of Darkness never revealed himself to me either – by choice). But insofar as this is Mr. Hide's story, other versions, other perspectives provided by their protagonists were not necessary. They will reveal themselves to the careful reader with great clarity and eloquence.

Whether or not this reflects the whole truth is fundamentally unimportant. It's what he wanted me to know, and as a deeply intuitive being, he gave a very full accounting. I hope you agree.

Part I

Leaving Michigan

Once upon a time, there was a young man. He was bright. He was good. He was sweet. He was special in a way one finds in children, for he had a heart that yearned to be whole. And he had a keen sense of his difference. He grew up torn, as we all are, between the desire to fit in, and the loneliness it brought with it, since fitting in means giving up the seeds of what makes us who were truly are.   But most important of all, his is a story of love – sought, found and abandoned – for all the wrong reasons.

He wandered through his childhood with parents who taught him little of any real use in life, except perhaps how to feign sincerity, being themselves more products of their own incompleteness, unhappiness and frustrations than of finding any fulfillment in their roles as mother and father. They had neither the time nor the inclination to help him understand. They were not bad people. In fact, they were quite ordinary.

His mother, an artist of emerging renown, yet self-effacing, with the typical mid-western way of women of her generation, working diligently to create her art. No explosive vision of a new world emerged from her, for she would never have authorized herself such power of expression, let alone imagination. But talent she had, and it was real, though in an almost craft-like sense. Art was to be applied for decoration not used for self-exploration. Such selfishness would have been a cardinal sin to be indulged in only carefully and indirectly.

The father, a man of no small ambition, yet of more limited ability, suffered his wife's success as if it was an accident designed to contradict his male dominance. His work was of a mundane sort, and in this typical male environment, self-expression was the last thing on anyone's mind. Rather, it was more about bluster, extreme positions, challenging – almost adversarial –

discussions designed to establish superiority rather than dialogue. Communication can serve connection, though when misapplied, can result in separation.

First in silence, then in outbursts of resentment rarely exposing his true feelings in this land of passive aggression, he ultimately struck a blow against the threat of being overtaken by a wife for whom he had little respect in either her person or her art. A mistress was taken. The marriage began to falter. And the first real battle in the larger war began.

But what of this boy growing up between two such parents? At the very least, his mother showed some interest in him, though it was through her art rather than through her love, as indirection was the prevailing syntax. His was also an artistic soul, quite possibly capable of far greater things than his mother, for his heart had not yet been frozen. He lived in a world of clarity – at least in terms of his vision and his sense of color. "Burnt Sienna" he asserted one day at school in art class to no small ridicule. "It's brown" insisted the teacher. Yet the boy stood his ground, sure of himself in ways which would too soon abandon him.

As a boy, destined to become a man, what did he learn from he who engendered him? He learned the cruder sides of men, more threatening than validating to a young soul such as his. And the place which should have been shared on the road to his own manhood was seized by a brother more in touch – or rather more out of touch – with who he really was beyond the identity of his gender. In spirit – if not in fact completely – he was cut loose from both parents, a small dinghy on the large waterless ocean that is the Midwest, to stare at the open horizon with no sextant to find or understand the stars – and most of all, his star.

With no guiding hand to point the way, he sought his path by looking to those things he liked to do. And to his surprise, he discovered that he was good at them. More surprising, he discovered that by following his own star, there was much he could achieve. Innocence prevailed – at least at first.

Sports were his first outreach, and where he applied himself, he excelled. Faith in his own abilities began to grow, though his parents neither participated in nor actively supported his efforts. Even in the face of external recognition, no value was placed on his achievements by those who, sadly, counted the most.

But it wasn't enough. He felt he needed more. Were his expectations set so high because no one helped him understand where and how to find them? In the absence of perspective, only absolutes exist. Did this mean that he could only fail? Or rather did it mean that these goals he set for himself were but substitutes for what he was really looking for? If this was indeed the case, what was his search all about? Inner needs go unmet and find temporary gratification only in deceptive illusions and misplaced beliefs. A pattern began to emerge. And along with it, so many questions.

Certain truths had revealed themselves to him along his way. Or so he thought, for when he was young, he often made judgements based on the need for an immediate explanation. Living with the uncertainty of unanswered questions was intolerable and he learned to transform them into ready answers more so they could be avoided rather than truly asked.

Caught in the middle of a divorce, one parent seemed to wither, ironically creating a vacuum stronger than the countervailing force of the father, who saw this conflict – as he did everything in life - as more a power struggle reflective of his own insecurities and frustrations than any positive lesson he could provide his son. Blackmail became the currency of their exchange, and seemingly neither parent rose to the task. A fatal rift was created between father and son – an unbridged void - destined to change the course of the boy's life.

"Take my side and I will support you. Stand with your mother, and you are on your own." This was the father's defining currency, consolidating a conflicted relationship into an outright struggle. And worse still, it set the boy's relationship with money on a much distorted path. The boy seized his independence firmly with both hands, more out of opposition than affirmation, as the man he was becoming, determined – as never he had done before – to stand his ground and fight for himself. He would fend for himself come what may. "No" was his reply, though the succinctness reflected the reactive nature of the response rather than any deeper sense of what had actually transpired. Gut reactions became his way of dealing with emotional conflicts – another fold in the fabric of his life was set.

Though he was successful, the foundation of his security was taken from him by an angry, controlling father, and the first bricks of a new, much darker edifice – perverted by this paternal betrayal – were laid.

Mother remained in touch, supportive, but caught in her own turmoil, touched by a debilitating disease which robbed her of one outlet – her art. The boy found no source of strength in his origins, and began his life as an adult on unreliable ground. And oh so many questions

Let down by both, he found himself adrift with a profound conflict he neither understood nor knew how to address, let alone resolve. And in the midst of this turmoil, the pattern was set. When situations became emotional, he was quickly overwhelmed. Lacking the tools – and he never sought them out – to make sense of conflict only one response emerged, his approach became one of flight – first through trivialization, and when all else failed, by complete avoidance. Thus was born Mr. Hide.

In his imperfect world, there was no Dr Jekyll to provide a counterpoint to the demonic other half. Indeed, having even a "negative", firm yet clear, can provide a from which useful counterpoint against which to set one's course. Ironically, his father served as this negative pole, determining so much of Mr. Hide's future bad choices. When he thought he was rejecting his father's influence completely, he was actually embracing his darker side and siding with his father's negative perception of his son. When there is no Sun, there is always a Moon.

No – young Mr. Hide was the unfinished amalgam of a disillusioned childhood and the chain of setbacks to come – none of which was ever really understood in a purposeful way. In fact, he convinced himself that even in the face of all that had happened, his existence was actually quite special, if not normal. Cling to the appearance of normalcy as a reliable bulwark against all that wasn't working. Smile when you are in pain. Ignore the obvious. It was all starting to come together. Mr. Hide's guide to successful living – chapter 1.

Yet deeper down, life made no sense, or the sense it made was too harsh. And to search for it became yet another exercise in frustration. With only a rejecting hand to guide him, he unwittingly sought out, and was to be easy prey, for others even more damaged and disillusioned than he.

"Each day is a new day" – a favored homily he often told himself after a setback, yet one which brought little real solace and certainly no cure. Each day wasn't so new, for the baggage was never lost nor set aside, let alone opened. It just grew bigger, heavier, and more difficult to ignore.

Yet this was a boy with inner resources, and a good – albeit by now wounded - heart. After one false start in a career he was not cut out for, he set his sights elsewhere, more in tune with his artistic temperament, for he felt he was more his mother's son than any descendant of the father he had come to despise. But there is always a cost to such rejection, for it comes not from a true antipathy, but rather from a sense of rejection, and a desire for healing, for some acceptance which is too threatening, too unattainable to hope for. There was a cost to declaring himself a fatherless child, though the deeper implications would confirm themselves over time, in the big city and its undefined promise of a new beginning.

Life in Manhattan, for this was an adventure lived in only the "best" borough - for with his new direction also came a certain pretension - was not what he had expected. Neither fame nor fortune come as easily as the young expect. Worse still, no love – even the easy kind young men mistake for the real thing – came to him.

In his own words, and from behind a mask of self-deprecation designed to somehow negate his own frustrated longing, the young man from the Midwest would say "….I can't even get laid." And he didn't know why. He thought there was something wrong with him, something missing, and so he retreated deeper into a façade reflecting the world he lived in, not realizing that the temporary success it seemed to bring was actually a promise of future alienation.

Venality, perversity, mistrust and perhaps worst of all, artifice, became the means for survival. Style replaced substance, and the link between his inner self and the required façade was severed. Doubt transformed hope into compromise, and reality itself was redefined in the language of the artificial world he inhabited. Money was earned by creating an illusion – in fact it had become his profession. Creativity was fueled by self-indulgent excess. And the rules – even the concept of rules – grew more and more foreign as he observed the perennially insular world around him. It all made less and less sense, but rather than question it, he pushed himself further, harder, to adapt.

Money existed to be spent in the most conspicuous ways, to further reinforce the mask. And the boy – now a young man – grew more deeply confused the more he followed these rules. He convinced himself that he had figured things out, becoming more cynical with each indulgence. "If I'm wearing the latest Calvin's then I'm living like Calvin, and since he's rich and successful, well, so am I."

Over time, the mask became the boy, who could not envision living without it. And his life became a series of "new looks," new clothes, new friends – substitutions for the real thing which he had begun to believe didn't really exist

Distractions came in many forms – all of them fleeting and superficial, their benefit never enduring. Fame came only to those who won, not to those who played the game with any true purpose – or so he thought. And he never really understood what it meant to win. People, even those who were successful, were so for only a time, to be regularly discarded in the constant need for the next new thing. And love – as always, proved to be the big loser – though in ways as yet little imagined.

He entered this world enthusiastically, posing as he was taught, believing that it would bring him what he wanted. But he had never stopped long enough to ask himself what it was that was really missing. All he knew was that something was missing. And so he redoubled his efforts, though misguidedly within his new paradigm. Yet the hole in his heart was growing, and it became ever more difficult to ignore the void inside. He was keeping too busy in this world of superficial values. Like some speeding car, the boy believed that if he kept moving, what he was running from might not catch him. Somewhere however he also knew that he was running from himself. He had made his choice. From a victim to a volunteer – a transformation had begun.

Lost and confused by what he saw, yet fearing to look inside, he embraced this external world based on emptiness, a world where the light which had been born within him would be devoured by a growing darkness. Loneliness took root and would grow with only cynicism to give it

meaning. The boy could control its effects for a time. But there were anxious moments when the sense of loss, confusion, frustration, and this unnamed longing would seize him. And in those moments, he would raise the volume to drown out these thoughts. Like some perverse metaphor, an evil pun, an emptiness filled him and drained his heart. This was the domain of Mr. Hide, and the boy embraced him all the more fully, for in fact, he feared to face himself. Mr. Hide, hiding from himself.

How does one respond to this kind of emptiness? The pain, like a hunger of the soul, requires a meal. Without understanding – indeed by rejecting his deeper appetites, his true needs - he fed in the wrong places. He let others in, believing that by opening himself in this way he could somehow absorb the qualities of those he had abandoned in himself. Like early man who ate a vanquished enemy's heart to absorb his courage, or his brain for his cunning, the boy turned the tables, ingesting what he thought would fill him by allowing others to feed on him. The reversal was advancing quickly and the transformation progressed. And by believing that he was making no commitments, he thought he didn't need any when in fact, that's exactly what he was searching for.

How ironic, for each fed on the other, believing that somehow they were getting what they needed. Everyone took. No one gave. And this pointless exchange further emptied his heart. But the loveless repetition was proof that there was no nourishment to be found here. He lived on a diet of human junk food – appealing at first, but full of empty calories and devoid of any real nutritional value. And what did he learn? Only that feeding delayed the next meal. And that no one was ever truly sated. Only one meal can satisfy this hunger, and the more he longed for nourishment, the more he came to fear it.

Mr. Hide had started to see the world in strange, new ways where his compromises would affect a momentary sense of pleasure, only to see it fade quickly. He tried to believe that this was all there was – a convenient explanation for which he sought and found support in the friends he chose. Though deep inside his heart knew that this growing darkness was consuming him, he had come to fear his own true desires for they challenged his pact with the devil.

What was this darkness that was engulfing him? How does one define such obscurity? To what purpose does it labor? What are its means? And of greatest concern, how might it end? All worthy questions, yet antithetical to the man he was growing to be.

For a time, he knew some success – due to his own talent, but also from frequenting others who were successful.   He believed that it could be contagious, only to learn that alone its symptoms are such. Success, when it smiled on him, was inebriating. But it proved fleeting and difficult to replicate for it relied more on external forces than what resided within himself. It was followed by periods of failure and disappointment.

It is always difficult to understand why at one moment we are embraced and another rejected when we are always the same. As the setbacks continued, and in spite of all the explanations he offered, fundamentally he blamed himself for his failures. In moments such as these, perspective is lost, and the reasons for failure are many and not always our own fault. But in Mr. Hide's world of takers, he had no one in his life who truly cared, no one who could both explain what had happened and give him the support he needed. In closing his own heart to himself, he had closed it to others as well.

Opportunities were offered, and taken, causing the waters of chance to rise and the cross currents of life to grow stronger, more agitated. And as his boat rose in these turbulent seas, he had neither time nor guidance nor sincere inclination to learn how to navigate them. To do so would open him up to those gnawing questions. His system began to falter. Not every truth can be transformed into a lie.

And the fall came. And it came again. And again.

Did he learn from life's lessons with the passage of time and the accumulation of experience? Was each reversal a setback, a fall from which to recover, strengthened and wizened by its very fact? Or was it felt as defeat, a message from life that good things were not really meant for him? For the boy, it was more the latter, as a growing sense of defeat began to spread, like the cancer it was. Though denied – as always - on the surface, its roots were deep, and their hold on his spirit darkened his light.

He let the darkness in out of guilt, for he knew that he had wronged himself. Things became confused as his heart and his head no longer spoke to each other. Change course, tack closer to his own true winds, and all his compromises, his false beliefs, the very edifice of his persona would crumble. Stay the course, cling to the sinking ship, embrace the emptiness and the sense of failure and the horrible loneliness grew. The latter, however dark, was at least familiar territory and made sense in his distorted world view. The former frightened him more, for it challenged his interpretation of experience and pointed him in directions unknown. A change of course was required in Mr. Hide's Odyssey, and a hero was needed. But heroes are not born. They are made. And Mr. Hide had no one to help him.

How to deal with such a lethal message, for even the most successful of lives contain their share of reversals? Would it cause him to build a stronger boat, find a more accurate compass to ply the waters of his life? Or would he build a place to hide, a stronghold which would keep the demons out – though deep in his heart, he knew they were the result of his pact with the devil? Unwittingly, unpreparedly, unknowingly, and under the tutelage of Darkness, his newfound friend, his teacher, soon to be his maker, the shadows grew longer, the light began to flicker.

What would become of him in the real world? Which path would open the door to the longed for success and recognition – these acclaimed substitutes for what he really wanted? Could he believe again in himself? Dare he? Would it be worth the risk? What would become of him if he set aside the entire edifice he had built in favor of a new beginning? With the dimming light, his vision failing, the path seemed more threatening than before.

The unknown terrified him for he had never found his courage – only his reactive rage and the pain that provoked it – to defend himself. The true unknown was not the future, but himself. And the less one knows oneself, the more of a stranger one appears to be. He saw his true self as the enemy, out to burn down his house and destroy his world when in fact, that is what he needed. And that is exactly why, against all logic, he fought himself with all his strength.

Another force had entered his life, one which would fit his particular pattern and set the tram for the coming years. For Mr. Hide, it was the Father whose betrayal early on laid out this troubled course. Indeed, all children need a Father. Some are lucky, and theirs is a force for good, for order, for strength and courage. They guide you, encourage you, and pick you up when you fall. And when we are afraid, they are there to protect you. Others are far less fortunate. But whether or not one has a father, the fact of the Father constitutes not only a fact, but also a challenge – to fulfill the confidence he may place in his child, a joining, and a shared sense of purpose. Or if he has failed in his role himself, a greater, darker more dangerous task: to lead the child to search out his own way home alone and with no compass to ply the waters of his life.

When driven by darker needs, darker solutions take hold. Every journey begins with its first steps and as the boy's father brought no light, he had no means of knowing how to choose one who could. Though he acknowledged always looking for "a coach," he had no model other than his own failed father to inspire his selection.

No – a Master of Darkness, a greater victim, a Lost Lord of the Shadows himself found the boy and took him in. He offered him a safe haven. He offered him a home. He offered him an identity and what appeared to be love – but which was, in fact, something else.

And so began a journey of discovery built on deception, disillusionment and disappointment – all transformed in this world of Darkness into their human forms of selfishness, self-indulgence and superficiality. Darkness taught a gospel of despair, thinly veiled, but sufficiently disguised so that those participating in its rituals could sustain the illusion of a different, more "realistic" – though actually cynical - vision of the truth. Its ultimate purpose? Apocalypse – for when there is no faith in oneself, one has no faith in the world. No hope, no brighter future exists. And worst of all, no love is to be found in this theology for all its saints share one thing – a profound sense of loss and loneliness. It's endpoint? Where it all began for the Master: alone and abandoned in this cruel world through no fault of his own – the core belief and his dark Gospel.

The boy, our Mr. Hide – had found the High Priest in the Church of Darkness, and now served at his altar. At first innocently. But over time, as his complicity grew, the boy came to recognize more clearly where this was going, even if he was too frightened to acknowledge where it might end. He had become a hostage and came to believe he had little choice but to embrace his captor.

And what of love, the source of light and hope? Had he ever really known love – or just its empty cousin, sex? Had he learned anything of love during his young life? No – there were no stories of romance or caring in his testament. Worse still, what could he learn of love from his dark teacher? Only what he himself had learned – that love is an illusion, and to search for it only leads to disappointment, betrayal and pain. Love, he taught, was to be held in contempt, for to believe in love is to believe in a false God. And the boy listened and began to believe.

Did the boy understand that love breeds hope and faith, the very essence of his strength, his courage, his future? Had he learned as he acquired new experience? Or, desperate for love and sustenance – emotions he kept carefully in check - had he so drunk so deeply from the wrong cup as to have lost his ability to believe? Had he mistaken – in the absence of light - release and perversion for caring and connection? The Master, Darkness, for that is how he came to be called, had initiated a process of transformation where the young man's very perception of the world would become reversed. Was he being literally reborn in his maker's image, unbeknownst to him – at least at first?

But a Light such as his is not so easily extinguished, and there were moments of rebellion against the darkness. Attempts were made to build protective walls to keep the darkness out believing that the harm came from the outside when it was really eating him within. Passivity, isolation, loveless sex and alcohol – all became the tools of Darkness. And as the walls grew higher, the light grew dimmer. But it never went out.

And one day, in a fit of unstated rage, Hide cast the Master out from the lair they shared. His one arm against which Darkness had no shield was his light – if only he had the courage to use it. Our Mr. Hide sought refuge with younger friends, seeking out the lost simplicity of his own fading youth, still unable to embrace his latent maturity.

But the souls he found were just as lost as his. He did abandon his dissolute habits activated at his latest setback, and sought out other positive remnants of his youth – notably in sports. It had worked then. Perhaps it would work again. But Darkness, like the insubstantial force that it is, found his way back inside, insidiously, perniciously and with subtlety, reclaiming in small, imperceptible steps, his place in Hide's world.

And those protective walls? Their purpose became clear only over time. In a perverse reversal of the natural order, what was to keep the enemy out, ensured that it would remain within. And the Light, now the enemy, was never to be admitted. Over time, the inversion took hold and Hide became confused – Light was seen as darkness, and Darkness was seen as all there was. Though his heart still lived and the light burned on.

In his daily existence, in his compromise, Hide ignored one thing in his efforts at self-preservation: walls – even protective ones – cast new shadows. And he woke one day to realize that though his castle provided some security, it had become a prison from which he dared not leave. His safe haven had become his cathedral of doom jointly held by its two lonely acolytes.

The price for security was indeed high. He would spend his life in the shadows, living alone, filling it as best he could as his options, like the tide, receded, and his courage with it. Or such was his vision of the future. A growing sadness took hold of Mr. Hide, for his heart had preserved something of itself, and unbeknownst to him, all the good things in himself which he had shut away, cried out for freedom and expression.

And then, through an act of merciful fate, he met someone new, someone from his past who, without life's intervention, he would never have met again. Different in every way from Darkness, love erupted in both their hearts. His light began to shine again. He started to see life differently. And he started to believe once again. So began a great struggle.

At first, he hid his love from the Darkness, for in truth, he had become his servant, and the Master would not have approved. He would steal away from his normal routine, adding a few hours before or after to spend with his love and his own Light. Only when he felt strong enough, or so he thought, did he confront Darkness, asserting his right to the Light – for that is what we can now call her. The boy had feared revealing his secret and mistook his Master's lack of reaction as a sign of acceptance. But this was not the case. Odd how even a little light, his light, blinded him to what he would have surely known had he remained in obscurity. Darkness feigned retreat, for directness, openness, clarity were not his way. And so slowly, stealthily, through indirect suggestion, he began his reconquest.

Hide felt joy. He felt love. He felt a new strength, and he began to imagine life in terms of new initiatives that he might take to dismantle his prison and climb out of the cruel shadows of failure and disappointment. Mr. Hide discovered that he could care, telling his love "….today, let me take care of you…." Such a simple statement of caring came naturally – and for the very first time in his life. He discovered that the encroaching numbness which had been engulfing him had an antidote.

Yet fear was never far away. He would make brave statements: "I will always be coming through your door" he told his love. And he would make darker ones too: "I am so afraid I'll fuck this up." Intuition exists and reveals to us what we'd rather not know. But Mr. Hide could speak his truth when they were together – proof of what was possible. In those moments, however, he could forget what would happen when he was alone. A breach had appeared, but it would prove to be self-healing.

These victories were never allowed to congeal into something solid, as the Master's counterattacks increased in intensity as the true nature of the threat became more clear. Never in the past had Hide opposed Darkness openly. That had changed. As astute observer of the weakness in others, Darkness never spoke of their growing discord. His quiver was never empty, however, of his favored arrows: guilt, doubt, fear and insecurity. Hide's father had laid a solid foundation. Darkness knew that to even suggest an imposition of paternal authority, his protégé's most well practiced reflex, would only result in furthering his rebellion.

No, Darkness sowed seeds of doubt: abandon his security, trust in the unknown, and believe in the Light when he had learned that only Darkness – and its Lord - could be counted on. Could anyone ever be trusted enough to give up what Darkness provided. To step into the unknown, to risk it all? For someone as unsure as Hide, such a wager would be simply unconscionable.

So Darkness tempted Hide with new projects which he knew would surely flatter him – yet another point of vulnerability. And when all was ready, when the pieces had been put in place, the final battle loomed on the horizon. He waved the specter of financial ruin and the loss of the one point of safety Hide knew – his home.

Hide fought for his heart, he fought for his life and he fought for his love. But he fought in silence, never giving voice to his own voice when and where it counted. First, his words grew empty, promising that which he knew he couldn't deliver. Next came silence, indirection and ultimately avoidance. All were part of his childhood legacy. Without words to give purpose and meaning to what he felt, Mr. Hide began to falter. He was not strong enough, he forgot the power of his Light, and most of all, the Master knew his victim well.

The Darkness had a varied and deep arsenal of insidious weapons, none of which would be spared. There were the first years together when he was boy and was alone (what looked like gratitude but was really guilt), unloved and abandoned – a prime candidate for the conversion. There was the pity, knowledge of Darkness' suffering – perhaps Darkness' greatest weapon.

And there was Stockholm – when a captive bond with their captor as the new source of security – somehow seeing his own struggle falsely mirrored in that of his as yet unacknowledged master. He felt needed, as Darkness wove a web of inextricable co-dependency, feeding the illusion – and even providing an opportunity for the boy to feel strong - when in fact, theirs was an unholy bond based on shared weakness only appearing to be something other than it was. Oddly, Darkness needed no strength, for he feeds on weakness, and his power grew with the destruction of HIde's belief in himself. Like some broken vessel, once drained of his courage, there was little resource left to nourish a true rebellion.

And what of the Light – his love? What were its arms? How do light and darkness engage? How is each battle's outcome determined? And what was the Light's true purpose, for the obvious always hides some secret.

What is the Light? Why does it exist? Though it presents itself as all the things the Darkness is not – love, caring, enlightenment, growth – it too has its roots in the dark soil from which it emerged so long ago. Are Light and Darkness but two sides of the same thing? And if so, what is that thing that gave rise to both and which defines neither?

Like the sun moving across the land, or the night spreading its veil of darkness, their succession seems inevitable and irreversible – indeed necessary. Though partners, they can never cohabit for long the same place, and only in those transitional moments, like dawn and dusk, are their mutual truths more fully revealed.

The sunshine warms, stimulates, forcing things to grow and be active. The night is for recovery, for rest, for restoration and immobility. We cannot spend all our time in one or the other. Uninterrupted light would burn and exhaust us. The night would lock us in a state of perpetual sleep. Progress comes from life's alternance. Yet the boy, seemingly condemned never to become a man, was trapped in the shadows of the prison he himself collaborated to build, hiding from the light, and stunted of growth.

Still capable of darker emotions, Mr. Hide felt guilt, of which he knew two kinds. The first was for the wrong he did to others, though his fragile sense of self forbade him any true or enduring remorse or apology – though it was transformed into more baggage and stored as more proof of his incapacity. To admit any wrong would be to question everything. In the absence of strength and courage, one can only think of oneself. It is of this that fear is born.

And he experimented with guilt, as much to learn about it, naïve as he was – like some stunted child - of its effects. On his love's birthday, they spoke of the future. And our no longer so young Mr. Hide – unprovoked simply, coldly stated: "You know, if it ever comes down to choosing between me and us, I will always choose me." It was almost diabolical in its banality. Though aware in a detached manner of what he had said, when challenged, his reaction was "…..are you breaking up with me?"

There was more here than meets the eye, for this was as much a test of his love's commitment as a sign of his failing courage. This man/boy, this innocent lost in his own selfish evil, was indeed trying to understand the forces at work within him. And they frightened him for only part of him was a willing participant in the journey of discovery.

And what of this second kind of guilt – the one we must all learn to know and fear. It is the wrong we do ourselves and is far more difficult to face, let alone resolve. When he looked in the mirror, his heart spoke its truth, and Hide knew that if he heard its voice, his life would have to change. So he shut down his ears, he looked away from his reflection, he banished the image Light offered him of himself, for though it was a beautiful one seen only through Love's eyes,

Mr. Hide had learned to fear any promise of a better world, for it was also the gravest of threats to the life he had built. Torn between the chance for something so much more than he had ever thought he could have and the fear of the change which it would require, the leak in his heart let his courage seep out rather than fill the brave vessel.

Change implies abandoning control, and Mr. Hide had long ago come to believe that he had to cling to whatever little control he felt he retained. Faced with such a choice and under his Master's assaults, he began to withdraw from the light, for it started to burn more than it warmed.

Truth was distorted into something more designed to conceal than to reveal. Words of explanation were to be avoided for to engage would mean loosening his grip on what was left of his unsettled reality. No discussion was to be allowed. Of necessity, this kind of guilt shrouded his eyes and welcomed the darkness. He looked into the mirror determined to see nothing of his heart.

Darkness fears above all else the burning light for its strength, its clarity, its purpose, and the longer it is withheld, for the creative destruction it ultimately unleashes. Like some vampire sleeping during the day, emerging only at night, all style and no substance, feeding off the living, and casting no reflection. Vampires do exist. They are not mythical creatures at all. They are created by others of their kind, older, more offended by the life they feed on, whose loneliness has driven them to engender new recruits, unnaturally, into their own kind. They live among us and go unrecognized by the living – until it is too late. Fear and Darkness. Courage and Light. How he wronged himself. After all, Mr. Hide had come to wear his name well.

But there were moments, wonderful moments when sincerity would resist all efforts at destruction. Separated for 10 days, Hide wrote his love "I miss you." Such an ordinary phrase, yet one he never let himself utter before – as if it was some suicidal confession. "And while you're away, when I'm missing you, I put on the sweater you gave me and I feel your warmth." Until then, the only sentiment Mr. Hide had allowed were words of self-indulgence for gifts which flattered his image – but never his heart. And the distance between them vanished in an instant.

But these moments grew increasingly rare as the subterranean battle raged.

Part II

The Light

The Light fought with its arms – love, faith, courage, honesty, openness, preaching authenticity to artifice, sincerity to the uncaring, truth to the lie – thinking to point the way. Yet unwittingly, it realized too late, these words of enlightenment blinded more than they illuminated. For over time, Hide's eyes had grown used to the darkness, and he found the light – though appealing – as he flew closer to it, too harsh for they revealed long forgotten truths. "Why are our conversations always so serious," he would ask, as the Light would shine its love on him. And the Light would respond…."Because you refuse to see." But saw he did, our Mr. Hide. And what he saw frightened him all the more.

If the Light is the source of knowledge, how ironic to discover its own ignorance, as human knowledge is that subtle blend of light and darkness revealing texture, purpose and deeper meaning. Truth resides only where both are to be found.

When they were together, "...it's wonderful." But when he was alone, the conflict raged in the form of voices whispering quietly at first, insidiously, in those moments of greatest vulnerability, mounting not only in intensity but also frequency as the battle endured. They whispered of danger, of risk, of an ill defined peril should he continue on his path to freedom. "Continue down this road and all could be lost."

What is this "all"? A fearful term, an emotional term, with neither true definition nor limit, promising annihilation, an end to those illusions with which we foster a sense of security. It is an absolute term, and one which allows no perspective. Lost perspective means lost faith in ourselves, and without it, there can be no faith in others. And all hope is lost. Like some frightened child, Mr. Hide the man, became once again the boy as he closed himself to the Light and abandoned himself to the voices he didn't know how to silence.

Why? So many facets to this question, but perhaps the most debilitating of all was his anger – for he was an angry child. And who wouldn't be? It would lash out from time to time – particularly with his father, ironically perhaps the only person with whom he truly shared strong, though resolutely negative, feelings. But his anger devastated him, exhausted him. His father treated his son as he did all men – as adversaries to be challenged. It was how he was raised, how men in his world interacted.

Yet Mr. Hide didn't understand this, having spent his whole life hoping for his father's love and never learning – as his brother had – that behind the gruffness and seeming rejection, an inarticulate, incomplete, unhappy man lived. He was a man who felt belittled by life, who had never found his own way forward, bitter from the sense of his unrealized – even if only imagined – potential. And he took it out on his son, who instinctively went where he himself could not go. He envied his son's future, for his had now become his past.

He nourished ambivalent feelings of pride and jealousy towards his son for Mr. Hide had come to New York and had "succeeded " in, if nothing else, leaving the town that was too small for him. The father – in his own failure of courage -had remained back home, resigned to a life smaller than he felt he deserved. Condemned to an early retirement, with too much time on his hands and too little inclination to make any real sense of his life, sharing a similar fate, their only connection was to fight – pointlessly – yet ritualistically, and on a regular basis.

And so was born a vicious circle of two blind men reaching out for each other, yet incapable of ever touching. A tragedy of truly Greek proportions with similar consequences for both. Mr. Hide the Man was still Mr. Hide the boy, desperate for his father's love and approval. And the cruelest irony was how this longing for love had been transformed into the one true conviction the boy held, one of the central tenets in the Church of Darkness: Love cannot be trusted and will bring only pain. Yet knowing he could never receive it, all that was left was his anger.   At least anger offered some sense of validation, some connection, even if all it really meant was yet another proof how deeply he had been wronged. Why does it hurt so much? Why feel anything if all it brings is pain? More from the Gospel of Darkness.....

Mr. Hide had other emotions too, but having no experience in dealing with them, he was quickly overwhelmed. For this was a young man with a heart, but a heart wounded too young, wronged too often that he no longer dared to believe. And the pain of not being able to find love – to give it and to receive it – had become too much to endure.

 Shutting down was the first line of defense, though it was only a stopgap measure. And when he was overwhelmed, all he felt was fear –

like pieces of himself being torn apart - disintegration. And when he was frightened, he would run away. Mr. Hide wore well his name. And who was always waiting to confirm how wrong he had been to believe in anything? Another object lesson from the Master.

During the months of struggle, the most feared question started to take shape for all concerned: could this war be won? How many battles must be fought? How long must the conflict endure? Will there be ongoing battles, skirmishes, and truces? Will it ever be over? And what emotions will rule for the fires of war are fed more by the unacknowledged heart than by the clear sighted head? Though love can be boundless, it can also have its momentary limits. And without failing, the Light would feel its own doubt born of pain rather than envy.

What would determine the final outcome? Could Hide truly face his fears, stare them down and say yes to the light – to his own light? Would his deeply buried desire to grow into his manhood emerge strong enough to prevail over the demon voices preaching security in stagnation? Or **can** the darkness of fear, the shroud of doubt, the specter of total loss – however improbable, be held at bay by the immaterial, and for the boy, unfamiliar and unconfirmed Light? Can shut eyes be forced open? Can blindness be reversed without the will to see? Does fear, like some blindfold, obscure that which even the brightest light has revealed?

As the war raged, and the Light – blinded by its own over-confident nature (a flaw it was reticent to acknowledge yet a necessary component of its own nature) – believed in the boy, and perhaps too deeply mired in its own role, ignored not only the strength but also the true purpose of the forces arrayed against it.

Is it possible that it suffices only to point the way? Or is it all one can ever do? Does even the Light have a blind side? Under the sway of its' own emotions, it too had become blind.

Talk of commitment was followed by missed appointments, itself succeeded by words of gratitude for holding fast against the doubt. After making love he spoke: "Now, nothing will ever come between us." Confusion deepened and his love's will was tested. Insightful yet blind, Mr. Hide's will eroded daily, until he created an incident, built on a lie, and announced that he could no longer endure the struggle. "When I'm with you, it's wonderful," was all he could say – leaving the rest unspoken. "I can't do this anymore." And as he was leaving, he offered yet again to meet and to speak – his heart still reaching out in spite of himself. Such was his dismay.

They met in a neutral place, a place where they had shared happier times together. But his love was resolved to launch its own counterattack. As Mr. Hide entered, his façade well consolidated. The light spoke: "What are you? Who are you? Are you some kind of lie?" Taken aback, his face went blank – yet opened. No defense was offered. He listened, was shaken, but though the door had not been locked, more than a foot had crossed the threshold of his prison.

Words of love – though of tough love this time – were exchanged, for though much was at stake, courage required resolve.

The next day, sweet words were exchanged, though not in person. But the distance was growing as the mortar dried.

What of this Light? By what law should it prevail, as it does in our favored fairytales? These stories we tell our children are not preserved across the generations because they are true. They are told because they portray some universal struggle each person must face, establishing the cast of metaphorical characters, each with its purpose, its strength, its flaws, and the prize. The struggle is one of endless variations, with as many possible outcomes. The pot of gold is never guaranteed. It exists as a promise for some future if the path is taken, if one endures the trials, and if one pays the price. Most important of all – and too often forgotten - it must be earned. Not everyone can find the means to be the hero. How different the world would look if it were so.

There was no absolute truth to be revealed here for both sides remain – the two sides of our existence. Only the broken topography of life exists, with its shifting perspectives, much like the shadows which lengthen and disappear as the sun moves across the sky. To find our way, our task is to assemble the sequence of images and turn them into something more complete and meaningful.

Life is a cycle where we begin our journey in darkness, our first reflex being to seek the light, relish its clarity, and learn of the world. Why do some see it bright and others dark? Do we carry the light within us? Can it be extinguished by circumstance? Do we ultimately decide ourselves through some inner truth which side we take? Or can the light conceal as much as the darkness – just differently?

The boy struggled in silence, used as he was to hiding his turmoil. This was what he had learned growing up in the hive, where his individuality was something at odds with his world, where emotions were the source of unresolved conflict, of weakness and vulnerability, a place where difference was the field of confrontation not resolution, and where innocence was bludgeoned by neglect. He never learned that his feelings were the very root of his courage, the compass of purpose, and the well from which he would draw his future strength.

Emotions are our first "thoughts" coming from our very essence with no intermediary of language, to be felt, and only then understood. They are perhaps the truest reflection of ourselves in the moment, providing both the direction and fuel for our efforts at establishing ourselves as separate from whence we came. Like thoughts, they are meant to grow and deepen, acquiring their own language as we interact with others. Shared, they find a true voice and become articulate. Ignored, they regress to a primal state, dumb and more reactive. Rather than propel us forward, they hold us back, locking us in an endless cycle of past wrongs that without understanding, we can never leave behind.

And what if one only learns to hide what one feels? How can one ever make sense of those very feelings? They remain like some foreign tongue overheard in the background, vaguely familiar and clearly relevant, yet beyond comprehension and therefore a source of misunderstood fear. Can a child ever learn to speak if it remains always silent? Frustrating these feelings become, because they are true in the first instance, not subject to our self-deception and therefore unavoidable - unless we seal them in some silent tomb.

Feelings exist for the very purpose of breaking the infernal cycle of self-delusion, of rationalization, which imprison them – and us. This conflict within himself raging, Hide – a man in aspect only - had to choose between two forces, neither of which he really understood.   But there was one with which he was far more familiar. It takes time and effort to learn a new language. Without it, our inner selves grow mute, contradicted and deeply angry, more capable of "no" and never "yes." Our Mr. Hide would have neither time, nor strength, nor more sadly still, will enough, to learn.

In spite of it all, the boy was brave, and went out into the world to meet with the Light, sharing there the joy of connection, the sense of fellowship and mutual understanding, and sensing in a new way what love can truly mean. He found a voice that came from within, and for the first time in his life, his body, his heart and his mind all spoke as one. And as he spoke, his words grew in depth, texture and wealth. But, like some prisoner only paroled, after his allotted time in the light, he would return to his den in the sky, where Darkness was always waiting.

Some days were good, but as time passed, he became less able to keep the forces pulling him in different directions apart. The Light offered to embrace the Darkness, to meet, naively believing that he might want the same things for the boy as the Light did. How foolish to think that the Master would free the boy simply out of love, for in the darkness, love does not exist – only possession. How blind was the Light to think that reason and the obvious could convince the Darkness that by saving the boy, he would also save himself. No. Darkness, true to his nature, saw the Light as the enemy, threatening his realm with destruction. He possessed the boy and would not give him up. There was to be no quarter.

Each wanted more of him, and caught in the middle, the boy got lost in the conflict of these two larger forces. A boy cannot make a man's choice, though a man he had become – at least in years.

A pattern had emerged within the boy which, in

time, had rendered permanent what should only have been temporary. Hide. Escape. Test. Flee. Hide. Escape. Test. Flee. Over time, would the cycle become truncated, reduced to its purest essence, eliminating with each round that which created the tension and provoked the aborted steps? Why submit himself to the inherent tension if it were to only end where it began? That would be a sorry end. Is hide all that would be left?

Part III

The Origins of Light and Darkness

In the beginning, there was Darkness, from which the Light emerged –though only after much struggle. They are not co-equal, as one resides on a deeper, darker, less accessible level. The Darkness emerged first from the chaos, living in the shadows, speaking in whispers, spreading doubt and fear, preaching avoidance, as was appropriate in the times when it ruled alone. That's why, when challenged, it is often the place we look to for protection. Love, courage, faith – these are things which took form and emerged only with the Light, and though powerful in their own right, require much to be possessed.

So it is, freedom from the Darkness can never come easily. Like some creature crawling out of the primordial slime, freedom comes only with great effort and conviction. Someone else can shine the Light, point the way, but until it is truly desired, found deep within oneself, until it is earned, it can be neither embraced nor possessed. It is a quest that fills a lifetime and gives it purpose.

And the light – what is its nature? It is so much easier to focus on the darker sides of things. How much does it hide in all its glare? Though it can warm and illuminate, it is often blind itself, flattening out the shadows and all that they contain. And it can burn, for most things we prefer not to see are purposefully hidden in dark corners and unused to the light.

Truth is more complex and textured than what the light alone can reveal. In its single mindedness, it can miss the subtleties which complete an image. Like much else in the universe, the light seeks its own truth, requiring some complement, and for that, it needs the shadows. Yet convinced of its correctness, it carries with it the seeds of its own limited vision. And it must fail – often multiple times – before it realizes that the compiementarity, that which can be gained by exploring its opposite, must express itself through conflict. And it can be just as stubbornly blind as darkness can embrace its obscurity.

But what of its own needs, for why would the Light not have needs as well? Indeed it has a purpose, a direction. Is something not missing? To what end would it serve to simply radiate warmth and caring into the cold, empty void? To be a sun with no planet to warm and nourish is not to be a sun at all. To truly fulfill its nature, someone must bathe in its glow. And a frustrated sun will struggle not to consume itself.

It strives to heal; indeed it needs to heal – both itself and the other – though of different ailments. How is that possible? Think back to the struggle to emerge from the darkness........though not clearly visible, there are many wounds acquired along the way. Scars may seal the skin and render it intact. But healing is not about the return to some pre-existing state. If that were the case, forgetfulness would suffice. No, true healing is more about growth, building on the pain and acquired wisdom. Like some tree whose limbs have been bent and maybe even broken. Yet to be itself, these wounds must form the foundation of a future not built on patterns that have long outlived their usefulness, patterns whose ability to protect now more serve moribund gods than seeds of a new future. They should be worn like medals – not hidden to feign some blessed existence spared of all trials.

The light can also doubt. It can discover its own brightness only when it can illuminate some treasure lost in the shadows. How odd that to be the light requires darkness, for light alone is nothing more than the opposite of obscurity, and can be just as lost. And when it is lost, without direction or purpose, what else can it do but doubt?

Needing each other, yet fearing each other – how perverse reality can be. Some might claim that this creates some vital tension, an impetus for constant movement, the opposite of stasis – an existential necessity. But until each finds the other or, worse still, when they lose each other, how painful it can be.

Darkness runs from its own truth seeking refuge in illusions, lost in a word of dark shadows and obscure voices. Light stumbles blindly seeing only length and width, but no depth. Is this really the motor of life? Or is it rather in the struggle to find the other – each lost within its own blindness – that some degree of clarity emerges. How wasteful. How cruel. How chaotic. Is there no better way? Is fate also blind, and if so, then fate is not fate after all, for in its' lack of vision, how can it decree any outcome?

And so does paralysis ensue as the logical consequence of fear? Is building defensive walls the only answer? Or is rushing ahead, believing that we will find what we seek when what we seek flees from us, fearing annihilation from union, the true path? Does the light pursue the darkness? Could the darkness pursue the light to some better purpose or must it be only to snuff out the light?

All we can be sure of is that both will be true to their natures and their purpose. So where can they meet? Is it just at those moments of dawn and dusk, of fleeting intersection? Would union mean the end of both? Or is it rather the beginning of something new? Is life an infernal chase? Or can this connection somehow endure?

Is there some third force at work here, *some dark matter* which we cannot see, capable of breaking down the doors the past has closed, clearing a path to the future? Can the past, and its demons, be banished forever**?** Such a big word – forever. Though its human significance is ephemeral, indeed impossible, it is what we all strive for. We call it love and proclaim that it can conquer any foe. But look around. Like some battlefield scene, one sees more victims than victors. And the wounded are everywhere.

What is love? We use the word as if we know what it means. From where does its strength derive? Its components are clear: attraction, sensuality, courage, and union with the other - a desire to be more than one can be alone. Many have abandoned the search and have reduced it to a set of neurochemical reactions. Others consider it to be some primal force, some biological imperative, that drives us to procreate. We create new words to disguise our ignorance and incapacity for that which we can't explain.

Neurochemistry is a dead end, and thoughts of procreation are secondary when love is present. No, love is about transcendence, about leaving one's singular self and joining with something bigger, something more complete, something which escapes the confines of the moment. It can even be someone....for sometimes the former is easier than the latter, easier to manage.

It is this hunger for completeness which drives us all, though it may take many forms – power, wealth, domination, codependency. All offer some promise of transcendence, though in each we've come to see their flaws and weaknesses. Only love can endure because it requires only the presence, the willingness, the desire for the other. Yet love too can go badly wrong.

When the other fears more for their own sense of self than they believe – they trust – in completeness with another, they retreat to that place of Darkness. Such doubt is the fruit of past experience which itself is the expression of a tragic pattern set early in life. To get past it requires a conversion, a spiritual experience that opens the door. But like all conversions, the door can only be opened from the inside. One must walk through it oneself.

Love is an act of faith. And without faith – mostly in oneself but also in the other - there can be no love. Cynicism is the final bulwark against emotion, disqualifying, mocking, trivializing emotion. It is the hiding place of cowards, the source of lies, the voice of a silenced heart and a virulent cancer starving its host until the healthy organs wither from neglect, no longer able to fulfill their vital mission. Vanity is the mask behind which the cynic hides placing all stock in the little that he feels, he still believes he can control – fooling no one, least of all himself. And loneliness is the only currency left to spend on fruitless indulgences capable of providing only passing distraction, ensuring the absence of any faith or cure.

Innocence, hope, faith are all born of sincerity. But Mr. Hide's malady – at least for the moment, had progressed too far.

Six months passed as Mr. Hide hid. Messages were sent – poems for the most part - for Mr. Hide was a muse to his Love, and the heart speaks best in rhyme and image. Silence was his method, though as was pointed out, silence is also the cruelest of lies, as in its most brutal form, it denies the truth its voice. Love's heart bled though in a different way from Mr. Hide's. It didn't empty of its precious fluid for though it had been broken, it was still whole, and the love that flowed from its essence refilled the wounded vessel. Love fought for Mr. Hide. Love fought for itself, for why love if only to concede defeat to the darker forces of life?

One cold day of winter, chance brought them together. Mr. Hide agreed to meet, though it was clear that his mask was firmly in place. He looked thin, gaunt even, and hardened. He was met with a wave of emotion as his own words of love, the promises; the declarations – now denied as if never spoken and meaningless - were served up again to him in a fit of pain. Stone faced, yet with the eyes of a deer caught in the headlights, he kept repeating "I don't care. I don't care. I don't care." Like some religious chant, its' purpose was as much to keep love out as to hold his own demons caged inside. It was a reverse exorcism. These words were the well rehearsed, yet hollow lies with which Mr. Hide spoke his renewed truth. How empty, how cold they sounded: "I don't care. I don't care." Like some declaration of forced capitulatin they rang out, proclaiming just how lonely he had become.

Odd that it ended as it began – with an expression of caring – yet somehow reversed. Though this is what he longed for – to dare to care and be cared for – he turned them upside down, and his heart inside out. Mr. Hide was once again alone, a hostage in his own safe house. Safe? Or so he may have wished it to appear, though there can be no doubt he knew what he had done.

Love set aside its raging heart for a time, hoping that this would assuage the pain. But it came back. And in the face of what some might call obsession, it persevered, though in a different way. No longer was it the voice of unrequited love, of the hole which cries out from the void. A mission had taken shape, and as he often did, Mr. Hide saw what it was about. His salvation. Yet this too, as the challenge to his unnatural construct against any form of sincerity, he both recognized and feared it. Invoking his Master's defenses, and with hollow sarcasm, he ridiculed his own future. The time was not yet ripe. All that one could hope for is that someday, somehow Mr. Hide would let his light burn anew, and that the stunted fruit of his life would ripen in the sun. Time is all any of us have and things left too long in the darkness cannot forever avoid decay.

Love sought its own salvation as its own nature dictated. Rather than run from the challenge, it was embraced for the clarity and growth it could bring. Painful, solitary, difficult was the process. Communication continued – intermittently and as dictated by the heart – and almost exclusively in one direction. Yet even from his prison, and with no small ambivalence, Mr. Hide took nourishment from the few rays that pierced his dark abode.

Does this mean that the future awaiting Mr. Hide is as inevitable as it seems? Can or should nothing be done? Should the Light retreat back into its eternal – yet so impersonal – cycle, to watch, if not wait, for the sad outcome? Should it abide by Mr. Hide's cold directive – "Move on"? To what limits should one restrict oneself?

Yet caring exists – that word again. It endures. It is the Light's response to the Darkness' silence. It follows the Light's path, illuminating before and after the point where it now shines, but so much richer because it has seen into the shadows and understood what is at stake. It is the seed of life and knowledge placed in the dark earth, warmed by its very existence. It is more than just the promise of future growth as long as faith exists. It is the very essence of the Light. But it is only a promise of what might be. Promises are indeed meant to be kept.

Victim or Volunteer. That is Mr. Hide's choice. What he chooses will only be revealed in the living.

Part IV

Epilogue

Many days have come and gone

So much to be reflected on

The Light burns, hoping to heal

Rendering to life what the Darkness did steal

Love endures, though thrust down deep

A heart is too precious not to keep

Sunshine* will return as it must always do

To begin once again its life anew

A promise once made is a promise to be kept

Under some rug it never be swept

So look inside, let the wound heal

Rediscover your smile and once again feel.

*Sunshine was one of the terms of endearment used for Mr. Hide

Other PUBLICATIONS BY THE AUTHOR

Available on Amazon.com in paperback and ebook formats.

SIX YEARS – a condensate of life

After 30 years spent abroad, the author, a Native New Yorker, documents his experiences, observations and insights about how much the city had changed, and how much he had changed. A rare exercise in an honest examination of oneself and the place where we live.

IN THE SEVENTH YEAR

The Past is Gone, The Present is Fleeting, and the Future Remains to be Written.

The logical next phase of the author's return where he takes what he has learned, and tries to apply it to reestablishing himself in the city of his birth – all with surprising results.

THE LEFTOVERS OF GOD'S ANGER

The deeply tragic tale of a young man who was brought into this world by a mother who only used him to force the man she was dating, to marry her. Once achieved, this was a child who longed desperately to find a place for himself in this world, and who struggled mightily for 33 years until, as one b one the normal pillars of every existence tumbles, and he was left with nothing and nowhere to hide. A story of dignity, tragedy, and pain, all born because – irony of ironies – he was born with a strong and worthy heart. A cautionary tale for all of us that some are dealt an impossible hand, who struggle to live in spite of it, and who only need a hand extended to them. Sometimes that can come too late. But I remain

convinced, for someone who had nothing, whatever he got from me was more than he had ever hoped for.

THE PROPHET – Tales of dead ends and other perils

Immediately following the election of Donald Trump in 2016, a pall descended over the country, and in fact, the world. All politic aide, the psychological implications of someone so inappropriate for the position, and their consequences are deeply troubling. But the issue isn't him. He didn't elect himself. A significant minority did, and almost did again. How did this happen? The author offers his deep insights, derived from close observation, as his conclusion becomes unavoidable and inescapable – he is a caricature of us. It's time to hold up the mirror and have an honest discussion with ourselves – each and every one of us. Without that, no democracy, the experiment in self-governance, can survive.

DAWN OR DUSK – A time for Choices

Almost midway through the first half of the Trump Administration, the author revisits one of his core themes, i.e. the psychological state of the union. It is a call for all of us to pause from our daily racing around to consider where we are going. For if we just delegate, though it looks more like an abdication, the authority of governing ourselves to one man, the we no longer live in a democracy. If this sounds dire, the author presents it as but one option. That's the whole point of choices, and the responsibility we all have to not only make them, but take them seriously enough that we consider them carefully. And if we fail, to seek someone else to blame robs us of life's greatest reward. As odd as it sounds, to make a mistake, and then to own it, is the key to learning. To do otherwise is little more than a cheat.

THE PROBLEM WITH PROBLEMS – Volume I – Why we need to know why.

The first of two volumes dealing with the real issues that actually create the problems people deal with in their lives. But when we focus n the visible, the obvious, we set ourselves up to rationalize the very role we play in our negative patterns. From there, all we have to do is look around to find other people or things to blame for our setbacks. No matter how clear the role we play in our own problems can be, most of us will do anything but acknowledge we have done anything wrong. Yet, the only thing we have control over in our lives is ourselves. So why waste time and effort making believe we can change the things we don't have any real control over? It's the old debate between symptoms and causes. For we here in the US, where life is lived on the run, we prefer symptoms because we can put a name to them and 'treat' them, making them go away – albeit temporarily.

THE PROBLEM WITH PROBLEMS – Volume II – Why being right isn't enough.

The more I thought about the issues central to Volume I, I realized the problem was far greater and deeper that even I imagined. As I took a fresh look at past events in patients, friends and families' lives, the more it became clear to me what was really going on. As a very close friend of mine used to say about his own situation, "I can't get out of my own way.: Not long after, he 'accidentally'' killed himself.

CLARITY FOUND – Now What?

As the journey towards understanding continued, long held patterns began to lose their ability to confuse, to conflate, to displace the underlying currents, concealing them from consciousness. Unaware of what's going on, these legacies of the past can persist an entire lifetime, handicapping our ability to address the inevitable challenges in life. If we can't see what's really going on, where these repetitive patterns come from and why we continue to cling to them, how can we possibly affect a change. Due t a disconnect with or own unconscious, this ballet of the blind has no reason to relax its grip on us. The answer? Asking the hard questions, acknowledging the role we play in elaborating our own unhappiness, how we fail to recognize opportunities for change, and even when we do see them, our fear of seeing them for real – convinced they are so horrible, so terrifying – that the prospect of continuing to be stuck in place appears more desirable than the risk of the unknown of change.

COMING SOON:

A collection of almost 100 essays from my practice on a diverse range of subjects. Written in a clear, succinct prose, with only a few poems for emphasis, my hope is that they will be sufficiently accessible to get all of us thinking about our lives, our choices and our decisions on a level that will open the way towards understanding the unconscious and its role in our psychological equilibrium – the key to mental health.

www.ingramcontent.com/pod-product-compliance
Lightning Source LLC
Chambersburg PA
CBHW081408280526
45788CB00009B/3025